EASY GINGER COOKBOOK

50 UNIQUE AND EASY GINGER RECIPES

2nd Edition

By
BookSumo Press

Published by
BookSumo Press, a DBA of Saxonberg Associates
http://www.booksumo.com/

ABOUT THE AUTHOR.

BookSumo Press is a publisher of unique, easy, and healthy cookbooks.

Our cookbooks span all topics and all subjects. If you want a deep dive into the possibilities of cooking with any type of ingredient. Then BookSumo Press is your go to place for robust yet simple and delicious cookbooks and recipes. Whether you are looking for great tasting pressure cooker recipes or authentic ethic and cultural food. BookSumo Press has a delicious and easy cookbook for you.

With simple ingredients, and even simpler step-by-step instructions BookSumo cookbooks get everyone in the kitchen chefing delicious meals.

BookSumo is an independent publisher of books operating in the beautiful Garden State (NJ) and our team of chefs and kitchen experts are here to teach, eat, and be merry!

INTRODUCTION

Welcome to *The Effortless Chef Series*! Thank you for taking the time to purchase this cookbook.

Come take a journey into the delights of easy cooking. The point of this cookbook and all BookSumo Press cookbooks is to exemplify the effortless nature of cooking simply.

In this book we focus on cooking with Ginger. You will find that even though the recipes are simple, the taste of the dishes are quite amazing.

So will you take an adventure in simple cooking? If the answer is yes please consult the table of contents to find the dishes you are most interested in.

Once you are ready, jump right in and start cooking.

— BookSumo Press

TABLE OF CONTENTS

Any Issues? Contact Us

If you find that something important to you is missing from this book please contact us at info@booksumo.com.

We will take your concerns into consideration when the 2nd edition of this book is published. And we will keep you updated!

— BookSumo Press

LEGAL NOTES

COMMON ABBREVIATIONS

cup(s)	C.
tablespoon	tbsp
teaspoon	tsp
ounce	oz.
pound	lb

*All units used are standard American measurements

CHAPTER 1: EASY GINGER RECIPES

ASIAN GREEN BEANS

Ingredients

- 2 lbs fresh green beans, trimmed
- 3/4 C. reduced-sodium soy sauce
- 1 tbsp diced garlic
- 1 tsp diced fresh ginger root
- 1 C. honey
- 1 tbsp sesame seeds

Directions

- Get a saucepan and pour in some water. Heat it until boiling.
- Once boiling add in your green beans.
- Boil for 6 mins. Remove all water and run the green beans under cold water to stop the cooking.
- Get a frying pan and stir fry your ginger, garlic, and soy sauce until aromatic then add in your honey.
- Finally combine your cooked green beans and mix evenly.

- Toast your sesame seeds in a pan for a few mins. Then use as a garnish over your beans.
- Enjoy.

Amount per serving (8 total)

Timing Information:

Preparation	Cooking	Total Time
10 m	15 m	25 m

Nutritional Information:

Calories	178 kcal
Fat	0.2 g
Carbohydrates	45.4g
Protein	3.5 g
Cholesterol	0 mg
Sodium	806 mg

* Percent Daily Values are based on a 2,000 calorie diet.

Sweet Garlic Salmon

Ingredients

- 1 C. soy sauce
- 1 C. muscovado (dark brown) sugar
- 1 (5 inch) piece of fresh ginger root, peeled and diced
- 1/4 C. olive oil
- 2 cloves garlic, smashed
- 1 (3 lb) whole salmon fillet with skin
- 1 untreated cedar plank

Directions

- Get a bowl, combine evenly: garlic, soy sauce, olive oil, muscovado sugar, and garlic.
- Get a resealable plastic bag and put your salmon in it and cover the salmon with the contents in the bowl.
- Let the fish soak for 8 hrs in the fridge.
- Submerge a cedar plank in water for 30 minutes before you start to grill.
- Oil your grate and heat up the grill. Cook your salmon on the grill for 20 mins on top of the plank with the grilled covered.
- Enjoy.

Amount per serving (8 total)

Timing Information:

Preparation	Cooking	Total Time
10 m	20 m	12 h 30 m

Nutritional Information:

Calories	384 kcal
Fat	23 g
Carbohydrates	11.7g
Protein	31.1 g
Cholesterol	83 mg
Sodium	1885 mg

* Percent Daily Values are based on a 2,000 calorie diet.

Balsamic Tenderloin

Ingredients

- 2 C. balsamic vinegar
- 2 tbsps diced garlic
- 1 tbsp diced fresh thyme
- 1 C. olive oil
- 1 pork tenderloin, cut into 2 inch pieces
- 1/2 C. butter
- 1/4 C. packed brown sugar
- 1 apple, thinly sliced
- 1/4 C. dried cherries
- 1 tbsp diced fresh ginger root
- 1 pinch ground cinnamon
- 1 pinch ground nutmeg

Directions

- Blend: thyme, balsamic vinegar, and garlic together. While continuing to blend add in your olive oil.
- Get a resealable bag and put your pork in it with the contents of the blender. Let it sit in the fridge for at least 30 mins.
- Heat up an oiled grill (preferably) or a grilling plate to high. Cook the pork for 12 mins until fully done.
- Internal temp should be 145 degrees. After fully cooked wrap the pork in foil and let it sit for 12 mins.

- Get a saucepan and melt some butter in it. Add in your brown sugar and get it bubbly. Once bubbling add in: nutmeg, apples, cinnamon, cherries, and ginger.
- Cook for 6 mins until the apples are soft. Top your pork with this.

Amount per serving (4 total)

Timing Information:

Preparation	Cooking	Total Time
10 m	15 m	1 h

Nutritional Information:

Calories	536 kcal
Fat	31.3 g
Carbohydrates	45.4g
Protein	19.3 g
Cholesterol	110 mg
Sodium	239 mg

* Percent Daily Values are based on a 2,000 calorie diet.

SPANISH-ASIAN CHICKEN

Ingredients

- 1 (3 lb) whole chicken, cut into 8 pieces
- 1/2 C. soy sauce
- 3/4 C. distilled white vinegar
- 1 bulb garlic, peeled and crushed
- 2 tbsps thinly sliced fresh ginger root
- 2 bay leaves
- 1/2 tbsp black peppercorns

Directions

- Get a Dutch oven and fill it with: peppercorn, chicken, bay leaves, soy sauce, ginger, garlic, and vinegar. Get everything boiling then set the heat to low and place a lid on the pot. Let it simmer for 35 mins.
- Once 35 mins as elapsed take off the lid and continue cooking the meat until half of the liquid has evaporated.
- Strain the liquid into a jar or container and plate the chicken for serving.
- Enjoy with rice that has been garnished with the liquid.

Amount per serving (6 total)

Timing Information:

Preparation	Cooking	Total Time
20 m	40 m	1 h

Nutritional Information:

Calories	517 kcal
Fat	34.3 g
Carbohydrates	5.3g
Protein	44.2 g
Cholesterol	170 mg
Sodium	1363 mg

* Percent Daily Values are based on a 2,000 calorie diet.

DESSERT I
(YOGURT, PLUMS AND HONEY)

Ingredients

- 2 plums, pitted and diced
- 2 tbsps diced almonds
- 2 tbsps orange juice
- 1 tbsp honey
- 1 tsp minced fresh ginger root
- 1 tsp ground cardamom
- 2 scoops frozen yogurt

Directions

- Get a bowl, combine: cardamom, plums, ginger, almonds, orange juice, and honey.
- Enjoy this mix over the yogurt.

Amount per serving (2 total)

Timing Information:

Preparation	Cooking	Total Time
10 m		10 m

Nutritional Information:

Calories	128 kcal
Fat	3.3 g
Carbohydrates	23.6g
Protein	3.3 g
Cholesterol	< 1 mg
Sodium	< 19 mg

* Percent Daily Values are based on a 2,000 calorie diet.

Korean Style Dressing

Ingredients

- 3 cloves garlic, minced
- 2 tbsps minced fresh ginger root
- 3/4 C. olive oil
- 1/3 C. rice vinegar
- 1/2 C. soy sauce
- 3 tbsps honey
- 1/4 C. water

Directions

- Get a mason jar and combine the following in it: water, garlic, honey, ginger, soy sauce, olive oil, and rice vinegar.
- Place the lid on the jar tightly and shake the contents for 2 mins.
- Now for 2 mins microwave the dressing with no lid.
- Let the mix cool slightly then shake it again with the lid on the jar tightly.
- Place the dressing in the fridge to chill before using.
- Enjoy.

Amount per serving (20 total)

Timing Information:

Preparation	Cooking	Total Time
9 m	1 m	10 m

Nutritional Information:

Calories	86 kcal
Fat	8.1 g
Carbohydrates	3.3g
Protein	0.5 g
Cholesterol	< 0 mg
Sodium	361 mg

* Percent Daily Values are based on a 2,000 calorie diet.

DESSERT II (HOLIDAY BARS)

Ingredients

- 1 3/4 C. brown sugar
- 2/3 C. butter
- 1/4 C. molasses
- 2 tsps ground ginger
- 2 eggs
- 2 tsps vanilla extract

- 1 C. all-purpose flour
- 1 C. whole wheat flour
- 1 tsp baking powder
- 1/4 tsp baking soda
- 1 tsp salt

Directions

- Coat a baking pan with nonstick spray and then set your oven to 350 degrees before doing anything else.
- Get a bowl, combine: molasses, brown sugar, and butter. Then add in: vanilla, ginger, and eggs.
- Get a 2nd bowl, combine: salt, flour, baking soda, and baking powder.
- Gradually pour the dry mix in the molasses mix and combine it all together.
- Fill your pan with the dough and cook everything in the oven for 35 mins.
- Enjoy.

Amount per serving (12 total)

Timing Information:

Preparation	Cooking	Total Time
15 m	25 m	1 h

Nutritional Information:

Calories	278 kcal
Fat	11.4 g
Carbohydrates	41.5g
Protein	3.7 g
Cholesterol	58 mg
Sodium	354 mg

* Percent Daily Values are based on a 2,000 calorie diet.

EASY FISH CAKE

Ingredients

- 14 oz. crabmeat
- 1/2 C. light mayonnaise
- 1/4 C. minced green onions
- 1 tbsp diced cilantro
- 1 tbsp lime juice
- 2 tsps minced fresh ginger root

- 1/4 tsp hot pepper sauce
- 1/4 tsp salt
- 1/4 tsp black pepper
- 2 eggs
- 3/4 C. dry bread crumbs
- 1/4 C. vegetable oil

Directions

- Get a bowl, combine: pepper, crabmeat, salt, mayo, hot sauce, green onions, ginger, green onions, lime juice, and cilantro.
- Form this mix in 12 burgers.
- Coat each patty with beaten eggs and then bread crumbs. Then each one in oil for 4 mins per side.
- Enjoy.

Amount per serving (6 total)

Timing Information:

Preparation	Cooking	Total Time
10 m	10 m	20 m

Nutritional Information:

Calories	283 kcal
Fat	18.6 g
Carbohydrates	12.7g
Protein	15.5 g
Cholesterol	107 mg
Sodium	576 mg

* Percent Daily Values are based on a 2,000 calorie diet.

DESSERT III

(GINGER AND RHUBARB BAKE)

Ingredients

- 1 C. white sugar
- 3 tbsps all-purpose flour
- 1/2 tsp salt
- 2 beaten eggs
- zest from 1 orange
- 2 tbsps grated fresh ginger root

- 8 C. diced rhubarb
- 1/2 C. all-purpose flour
- 2 C. brown sugar
- 1/2 C. salted butter
- 2 tsps cinnamon
- 2 C. rolled oats

Directions

- Coat a casserole dish with oil and then set your oven to 350 degrees before doing anything else.
- Get a bowl, combine: rhubarb, sugar, ginger, 3 tbsps flour, orange zest, eggs, and salt.
- Blend the following with a blender: cinnamon, half a C. of flour, butter, brown sugar, and oatmeal.

- Combine both bowls then form a crust from the mix and pressed it down into your dish.
- Cook the mix in the oven for 45 mins.
- Enjoy.

Amount per serving (15 total)

Timing Information:

Preparation	Cooking	Total Time
20 m	40 m	1 h

Nutritional Information:

Calories	266 kcal
Fat	7.7 g
Carbohydrates	47.5g
Protein	3.6 g
Cholesterol	41 mg
Sodium	139 mg

* Percent Daily Values are based on a 2,000 calorie diet.

CURRY AND GINGER (DUMP DINNER)

Ingredients

- 1/4 C. all-purpose flour
- 2 1/2 lbs lean boneless beef chuck, cut into 1/2 by 2 inch strips
- 2/3 C. water
- 1/3 C. tomato paste
- 2 large onions, finely diced
- 3 tbsps grated fresh ginger
- 6 cloves garlic, minced
- 1 (2 inch) piece cinnamon stick
- 1 tsp ground turmeric
- 1 tsp ground paprika
- 2 tbsps ground cumin
- 1 tbsp ground coriander
- 1 tsp ground cardamom
- 1/2 tsp ground cloves
- 1/2 tsp ground cayenne pepper
- 1/4 tsp ground nutmeg
- salt to taste
- 1/3 C. diced fresh cilantro

Directions

- Get a bowl and combine water and tomato paste.
- Coat your beef with flour and then enter the following into your crock pot: beef, nutmeg, onions, paprika, ginger, turmeric, garlic, cinnamon stick, tomato paste mix, cayenne, cumin, cloves, cardamom, and coriander.

- Cook the mix for 9 hrs with low heat.
- Add in some cilantro and salt.
- Enjoy.

Amount per serving (10 total)

Timing Information:

Preparation	Cooking	Total Time
25 m	9 h	9 h 25 m

Nutritional Information:

Calories	170 kcal
Fat	7.2 g
Carbohydrates	9.4g
Protein	17 g
Cholesterol	53 mg
Sodium	226 mg

* Percent Daily Values are based on a 2,000 calorie diet.

Gari

(Canning Ginger)

Ingredients

- 8 oz. fresh young ginger root, peeled, chunked
- 1 1/2 tsps sea salt
- 1 C. rice vinegar
- 1/3 C. white sugar

Directions

- Combine your pieces of ginger with salt then let the contents sit for 40 mins.
- Now place the ginger in a mason jar.
- Get the following boiling, while stirring: sugar and rice vinegar.
- Once the mix has boiled for 3 mins and all the sugars have mixed evenly into the vinegar. Add the liquid to a mason jar.
- Let the contents lose all their heat without the lid, then place the lid on the jar and put it in the fridge for 5 days.
- Now once you see that ginger has turned pink remove it from the jar and cut the ginger into thin pieces.
- Enjoy.

Amount per serving (32 total)

Timing Information:

Preparation	Cooking	Total Time
40 m	5 m	45 m

Nutritional Information:

Calories	14 kcal
Fat	< 0.1 g
Carbohydrates	< 3.3g
Protein	0.1 g
Cholesterol	< 0 mg
Sodium	83 mg

* Percent Daily Values are based on a 2,000 calorie diet.

RUSTIC PANCAKES

Ingredients

- 3/4 C. milk
- 1/2 C. cold brewed coffee
- 1/2 C. butter, melted and cooled to lukewarm
- 4 eggs
- 2 C. all-purpose flour
- 1 C. whole wheat flour
- 1 1/8 C. light brown sugar
- 1 1/2 tsps baking soda
- 1 tbsp baking powder
- 1 tsp salt
- 1 1/2 tsps ground cinnamon
- 1 1/2 tsps ground ginger
- 1/4 tsp ground nutmeg
- 1/8 tsp ground cloves
- cooking spray

Directions

- Get a bowl, combine: eggs, milk, butter, and coffee.
- Get a 2nd bowl, combine: regular flour, cloves, wheat flour, nutmeg, sugar, ginger, baking soda, cinnamon, baking powder, and salt.
- Combine both bowls and mix everything until smooth. Let the mix stand for 20 mins.
- Fry dollops of the mix in a pan coated with nonstick spray until bubbles form then flip the contents and cook the opposite side for the same amount of time.

- Continue until all of the mix has been fried in this manner.
- Enjoy.

Amount per serving (6 total)

Timing Information:

Preparation	Cooking	Total Time
15 m	30 m	55 m

Nutritional Information:

Calories	580 kcal
Fat	20.1 g
Carbohydrates	89.8g
Protein	12.6 g
Cholesterol	167 mg
Sodium	1060 mg

* Percent Daily Values are based on a 2,000 calorie diet.

GINGER BEETS

Ingredients

- 6 medium beets, scrubbed and cleaned
- 1 C. orange juice
- 2 tbsps candied ginger
- 2 tbsps maple syrup
- 1/2 C. walnuts
- 1 tbsp white vinegar
- 1 tbsp cornstarch

Directions

- Submerge your beets in water, in a saucepan, and boil them for 50 mins. Then remove all the liquids.
- Peel off the skin of the beets and slice each one into wedges.
- Now place everything to the side.
- Add the following to the saucepan: orange juice, ginger, syrup, nuts, vinegar, and cornstarch.
- Now stir the mix and get everything boiling.
- Continue boiling the mix until it becomes thick then add in your beets and stir everything again.
- Enjoy.

Amount per serving (6 total)

Timing Information:

Preparation	Cooking	Total Time
10 m	1 h	1 h 10 m

Nutritional Information:

Calories	148 kcal
Fat	6.8 g
Carbohydrates	20.8g
Protein	3.1 g
Cholesterol	0 mg
Sodium	66 mg

* Percent Daily Values are based on a 2,000 calorie diet.

VIETNAMESE SOUP

Ingredients

- 2 tsps sesame oil, divided
- 1 (4 inch) piece fresh ginger, peeled and diced, or to taste
- 3 quarts chicken broth
- 1 large red onion, diced
- 2 C. sliced carrots
- 1 tbsp curry powder
- 1 tbsp ground ginger
- 1 tbsp cayenne pepper
- salt and ground black pepper to taste
- 1 jalapeno pepper, finely diced
- 6 limes, juiced, divided
- 1 (9 oz.) package udon noodles
- 4 skinless, boneless chicken breast halves, cubed
- 1 leek, cut into matchstick-size pieces
- 1 green onion, finely diced

Directions

- Stir fry your ginger in 1 tbsp of sesame oil for 12 mins, add in the broth, place a lid on the pot, and cook the mix for 35 mins.
- Add the carrots and onions and cook for 12 more mins then add: black pepper, jalapeno, curry, salt, ginger, 1/2 lime juice, and cayenne.
- Let the mix cook for 50 mins with a low heat.

- Boil your noodles in water and salt for 11 mins then remove all the liquids.
- Now stir fry your chicken in 1 tsp of sesame oil for 12 mins or until it is fully done then add the chicken to the broth mix and the green onions and leeks as well.
- Cook the mix for 13 more mins then shut the heat.
- Divide your noodles between serving bowls and add some broth mix to each as well as the rest of the lime.
- Enjoy.

Amount per serving (8 total)

Timing Information:

Preparation	Cooking	Total Time
15 m	1 h 40 m	1 h 55 m

Nutritional Information:

Calories	230 kcal
Fat	3.5 g
Carbohydrates	30.6g
Protein	17.9 g
Cholesterol	40 mg
Sodium	1696 mg

* Percent Daily Values are based on a 2,000 calorie diet.

PEPPERS, PORK, AND CHESTNUTS

Ingredients

- 2 tbsps soy sauce
- 2 tbsps cider vinegar
- 2 tbsps brown sugar
- 1 tbsp hoisin sauce
- 2 cloves garlic, diced
- 1 tsp salt
- 2 tbsps sesame oil, divided
- 1 1/2 lbs boneless pork chops, cut into stir-fry strips
- 1 red bell pepper, diced
- 1/2 onion, diced
- 1 (12 oz.) package frozen stir-fry vegetables
- 1 (8 oz.) can sliced water chestnuts, drained
- 2 tsps ground ginger
- 1 tsp red pepper flakes (optional)

Directions

- Get a bowl, combine: salt, soy sauce, garlic, cider vinegar, hoisin, and brown sugar.
- Add in your pork and stir the mix to evenly coat the meat.
- Let the pork sit in the marinade for 12 mins. Then being to stir fry the meat in 1 tbsp of oil for 4 mins, until fully done and then remove the meat from the pan.
- Add in the onions, bell peppers and more oil.

- Now cook the contents for 4 mins and combine in the water chestnuts, frozen veggies, pepper flakes and ginger.
- Cook the veggies for 7 mins then add the pork back into the pan and get everything hot.
- Enjoy.

Amount per serving (6 total)

Timing Information:

Preparation	Cooking	Total Time
20 m	15 m	45 m

Nutritional Information:

Calories	252 kcal
Fat	12.3 g
Carbohydrates	19.1g
Protein	17 g
Cholesterol	39 mg
Sodium	906 mg

* Percent Daily Values are based on a 2,000 calorie diet.

SOY DIJON TANGY DRESSING

Ingredients

- 1 C. olive oil
- 1/4 C. soy sauce
- 1 lemon, juiced
- 3 cloves garlic, minced
- 3 tbsps minced fresh ginger root
- 1 tsp prepared Dijon-style mustard
- 2 tsps honey
- ground black pepper to taste

Directions

- Get a bowl, combine: pepper, soy sauce, honey, lemon juice, mustard, ginger, and garlic.
- Now gradually combine in your oil slowly and keep mixing.
- Pour the entire mix into a mason jar and place the dressing in the fridge until the mix is completely cold.
- Enjoy.

Amount per serving (12 total)

Timing Information:

Preparation	Cooking	Total Time
5 m		5 m

Nutritional Information:

Calories	170 kcal
Fat	18 g
Carbohydrates	3g
Protein	< 0.5 g
Cholesterol	0 mg
Sodium	312 mg

* Percent Daily Values are based on a 2,000 calorie diet.

MAUI CHICKEN

Ingredients

- 1 tbsp sesame or canola oil
- 1 lb chicken tenders, cut into 1-inch pieces
- 1 (2 inch) piece fresh ginger, peeled and cut into matchsticks or minced
- 4 cloves garlic, thinly sliced
- 1/2 C. dry sherry (see Tip)
- 1 (14 oz.) can reduced-sodium chicken broth
- 1 1/2 C. water
- 2 tbsps reduced-sodium soy sauce
- 1 tsp Asian red chili sauce, such as sriracha, or to taste
- 1 bunch mustard greens or chard, stemmed and diced*

Directions

- Stir fry your chicken in a Dutch oven for 9 min.
- Then remove them from the pot. Combine in the garlic and the ginger and cook everything for 30 secs then add the sherry and fry the mix for 4 mins while scraping the pan.
- Now combine in the water and broth and get everything boiling with a high level of heat.

- Once the mix is boiling let it continue for 7 mins then add: chards, chili sauce, and soy sauce.
- Continue cooking this mix for 3 mins.
- Enjoy.

Amount per serving (4 total)

Timing Information:

Preparation	Cooking	Total Time
		35 m

Nutritional Information:

Calories	221 kcal
Fat	6.5 g
Carbohydrates	10.8g
Protein	26.6 g
Cholesterol	67 mg
Sodium	1048 mg

* Percent Daily Values are based on a 2,000 calorie diet.

Dessert IV
(Classical Muffins)

Ingredients

- non-stick cooking spray
- 1 C. all-purpose flour
- 1 C. quick-cooking rolled oats
- 3 tbsps packed brown sugar
- 1 1/2 tsps baking powder
- 3/4 tsp ground ginger, divided
- 1/4 tsp salt
- 2/3 C. fat-free milk
- 1/3 C. cooking oil
- 1 egg, beaten
- 3/4 C. diced pear
- 1/4 C. diced walnuts (optional)
- 1 tbsp oat bran

Directions

- Coat a muffin tin with nonstick spray and set your oven to 400 degrees before doing anything else.
- Get a bowl, combine: salt, flour, 1/4 tsp ginger, oats, baking powder, and brown sugar.
- Get a 2nd bowl, combine: eggs, oil, and milk.

- Combine both bowls to form a smooth batter. Then equally divide the mix amongst your muffin tin.
- Get a 3rd bowl and combine the rest of the ginger and the oat bran.
- Divide this mix between each section in the muffin tin as well.
- Cook in everything in the oven for 19 mins. Then let the contents sit for 7 mins.
- Enjoy.

Amount per serving (12 total)

Timing Information:

Preparation	Cooking	Total Time
20 m	20 m	45 m

Nutritional Information:

Calories	166 kcal
Fat	8.7 g
Carbohydrates	19.1g
Protein	3.5 g
Cholesterol	16 mg
Sodium	125 mg

* Percent Daily Values are based on a 2,000 calorie diet.

Dessert V

(Cinnamon Cookies)

Ingredients

- 2 C. lightly packed brown sugar
- 1 C. butter-flavored shortening, melted
- 1/2 C. unsalted butter, melted
- 1/2 C. molasses
- 2 eggs
- 1 tbsp baking soda
- 1 tbsp ground cinnamon
- 1 tbsp ground ginger
- 1 tsp salt
- 1 tsp ground cloves
- 1/2 tsp cayenne pepper
- 4 C. all-purpose flour
- 1/2 C. coarse sugar crystals, or as needed

Directions

- Set your oven to 375 degrees before doing anything else.
- Get a bowl, combine: cayenne, brown sugar, cloves, shortening, salt, butter, ginger, molasses, cinnamon, eggs, and baking soda.
- Now add in the flour and mix the contents.
- Shape the resulting dough into 48 balls then coat each one with sugar.

- To easily do this place some sugar in a bowl and after you form a ball roll it in the bowl with the sugar.
- Place everything on a baking sheet and flatten the balls into cookies.
- Cook everything in the oven for 10 mins in the oven.
- Enjoy.

Amount per serving (48 total)

Timing Information:

Preparation	Cooking	Total Time
20 m	10 m	30 m

Nutritional Information:

Calories	151 kcal
Fat	6.7 g
Carbohydrates	21.8g
Protein	1.4 g
Cholesterol	13 mg
Sodium	129 mg

* Percent Daily Values are based on a 2,000 calorie diet.

Ginger Loaf

Ingredients

- 2 C. all-purpose flour
- 1 tsp baking soda
- 1 tsp ground cinnamon
- 1/4 tsp ground nutmeg
- 1/4 tsp ground ginger
- 1/4 tsp salt
- 1/2 C. butter, softened
- 1/2 C. white sugar
- 1/2 C. brown sugar
- 2 1/3 C. mashed overripe bananas
- 2 eggs, beaten
- 1 tbsp lemon juice
- 1 tsp vanilla extract

Directions

- Coat a bread pan with nonstick spray and set your oven to 350 degrees before doing anything else.
- Get a bowl, mix: salt, flour, ginger, baking soda, nutmeg, and cinnamon.

- Get a 2nd bowl, combine: brown sugar, white sugar, and butter.
- Now grab a mixer and begin processing everything for 2 mins.
- Add in: vanilla extract, bananas, lemon juice, and eggs.
- Continue mixing everything until it is evenly mixed.
- Now combine both bowls and stir the contents until they are smooth.
- Place the mix into your bread pan and cook it in the oven for 1 hour.
- Enjoy.

Amount per serving (12 total)

Timing Information:

Preparation	Cooking	Total Time
15 m	1 h	1 h 25 m

Nutritional Information:

Calories	264 kcal
Fat	8.9 g
Carbohydrates	43.6g
Protein	3.8 g
Cholesterol	51 mg
Sodium	223 mg

* Percent Daily Values are based on a 2,000 calorie diet.

EASY GINGER SNAPS

Ingredients

- 2 C. all-purpose flour
- 1 C. white sugar
- 2/3 C. canola oil
- 1/4 C. unsulfured molasses
- 1 egg
- 2 tsps baking soda
- 1 tsp ground cinnamon
- 1 tsp ground ginger
- 1/2 tsp salt
- 1/4 C. white sugar, or as needed

Directions

- Get a bowl, combine: ginger, flour, cinnamon, 1 C. of sugar, baking soda, canola oil, egg, and molasses.
- Place the contents in the fridge for 1 hr.
- Now set your oven to 350 degrees before doing anything else.
- Get a 2nd bowl and add in 1/4 of a C. of sugar in it.

- Form as many balls from your dough as possible and then roll them in sugar.
- Place the balls on a baking sheet and then flatten them.
- Cook everything in the oven for 9 mins then let them cool for 15 mins.
- Enjoy.

Amount per serving (24 total)

Timing Information:

Preparation	Cooking	Total Time
10 m	10 m	1 h 30 m

Nutritional Information:

Calories	147 kcal
Fat	6.5 g
Carbohydrates	21.1g
Protein	1.3 g
Cholesterol	8 mg
Sodium	158 mg

* Percent Daily Values are based on a 2,000 calorie diet.

GINGER SAUCE FOR RICE

Ingredients

- 1/4 C. diced onion
- 1 clove garlic, minced
- 1 tbsp minced fresh ginger root
- 1/2 lemon, juiced
- 1/4 C. soy sauce
- 1/4 tsp sugar
- 1/4 tsp white vinegar

Directions

- Puree the following in a blender: vinegar, onions, sugar, garlic, soy sauce, ginger, and lemon juice.
- Enjoy over cooked jasmine rice.

Amount per serving (6 total)

Timing Information:

Preparation	Cooking	Total Time
10 m		10 m

Nutritional Information:

Calories	12 kcal
Fat	< 0 g
Carbohydrates	< 2.9g
Protein	< 0.9 g
Cholesterol	0 mg
Sodium	602 mg

* Percent Daily Values are based on a 2,000 calorie diet.

LEMON BREAD

Ingredients

- 1 C. water
- 1 tsp salt
- 1 1/2 tsps canola oil
- 1 tsp lemon juice
- 3 C. bread flour
- 1/2 tsp ground cinnamon
- 1 tsp ground ginger
- 3 tbsps white sugar
- 1 tsp active dry yeast
- 1/4 C. diced crystallized ginger
- 1 tbsp white sugar

Directions

- Place all the ingredients into your bread machine except the crystallized ginger.
- Set the machine to the dough cycle and let it finish.
- Take out the dough and knead it on a working surface coated with flour and then shape it into a ball.

- Place the dough into a bowl and place a towel over the bowl.
- Let the dough sit for 20 mins.
- Now get your crystallized ginger and knead it into the dough and place everything into the bread pan.
- Let the mix sit for 50 mins.
- Now set your oven to 375 degrees before doing anything else.
- Cut an incision into the top of the loaf and add in 1 tbsp of sugar.
- Cook the bread in the oven for 35 mins.
- Enjoy.

Amount per serving (12 total)

Timing Information:

Preparation	Cooking	Total Time
10 m	30 m	3 h

Nutritional Information:

Calories	153 kcal
Fat	1.2 g
Carbohydrates	31g
Protein	4.3 g
Cholesterol	0 mg
Sodium	196 mg

* Percent Daily Values are based on a 2,000 calorie diet.

POMEGRANATES AND PORK

Ingredients

- 1 (6 lb) 12-rib crown roast of pork
- salt and pepper to taste
- 1 C. orange marmalade
- 1/2 C. pomegranate juice
- 2 tsps diced fresh ginger root
- 1 lime, juiced
- 2 tbsps soy sauce

Directions

- Set your oven to 350 degrees before doing anything else.
- Coat your pork with pepper and salt and place it all into a casserole dish.
- Place the dish into the oven and let it cook for 95 mins.
- Get a bowl, combine: soy sauce, pomegranate juice, lime juice, and ginger.
- Get this mix gently boiling then add in the marmalade and place the contents to the side.

- Top your roast with 1/3 of the glaze and cook it for 9 more mins then add the rest of the glaze.
- Finally cook the roast for 10 more mins and check that the pork as a temperature readout of 145 degrees.
- Carve the pork before serving.
- Enjoy.

Amount per serving (8 total)

Timing Information:

Preparation	Cooking	Total Time
15 m	2 h	2 h 15 m

Nutritional Information:

Calories	503 kcal
Fat	22.3 g
Carbohydrates	35.7g
Protein	40.1 g
Cholesterol	119 mg
Sodium	609 mg

* Percent Daily Values are based on a 2,000 calorie diet.

HOLIDAY MORNING LATTE

Ingredients

- 1/2 C. milk
- 1/2 C. water
- 1 tbsp white sugar
- 1 tbsp instant coffee
- 1 pinch ground ginger
- 1 pinch ground cinnamon
- 1 pinch ground cloves
- 1 pinch ground nutmeg
- 1 tbsp whipped cream, or more to taste

Directions

- Get a bowl, combine: nutmeg, milk, cloves, water, ginger, coffee, and sugar.
- Place the mix in the microwave for 3 mins then enter it into a coffee C.
- Add your whipped topping and serve hot.
- Enjoy.

Amount per serving (1 total)

Timing Information:

Preparation	Cooking	Total Time
5 m	2 m	7 m

Nutritional Information:

Calories	138 kcal
Fat	3.7 g
Carbohydrates	22.2g
Protein	4.7 g
Cholesterol	12 mg
Sodium	61 mg

* Percent Daily Values are based on a 2,000 calorie diet.

GINGER SOUP

Ingredients

- 2 tsps olive oil
- 1/2 C. diced onion
- 1 large head cauliflower, cut into florets
- 3 C. chicken stock
- 1 (1 inch) piece fresh ginger, diced
- 1 1/2 tsps sea salt
- ground black pepper to taste

Directions

- Stir fry your onions, in oil, in a saucepan, for 2 mins then add in the cauliflower and place a lid on the pot.
- Cook the mix for 12 mins and after 6 mins stir the contents.
- Cook this mix with a medium level of heat.
- Now add in: pepper, stock, salt, and ginger.
- Get everything boiling then set the heat to low and cook everything for 35 mins.
- Let the soup cool for 5 mins then grab an immersion blender and puree the soup.
- Get everything hot again and serve.
- Enjoy.

Amount per serving (2 total)

Timing Information:

Preparation	Cooking	Total Time
10 m	40 m	50 m

Nutritional Information:

Calories	183 kcal
Fat	6.2 g
Carbohydrates	28.4g
Protein	9.8 g
Cholesterol	1 mg
Sodium	< 2477 mg

* Percent Daily Values are based on a 2,000 calorie diet.

GINGER SOUP II

Ingredients

- 3 tbsps butter
- 2 tbsps vegetable oil
- 2 tbsps minced fresh ginger root
- 1 tbsp all-purpose flour
- 1/2 tsp ground turmeric
- black pepper to taste
- 2 C. water
- 2 C. whole milk
- 1 tsp salt

Directions

- Stir fry your ginger for 6 mins in veggie oil and butter then add in the pepper, turmeric, and flour. Cook this mix for 2 more mins then add in the milk and water. Get the contents boiling, then set the heat to low, and gently cook for 4 mins while stirring. Once the mix is thick add in salt and strain it through a sieve.
- Enjoy.

Amount per serving (4 total)

Timing Information:

Preparation	Cooking	Total Time
10 m	15 m	25 m

Nutritional Information:

Calories	221 kcal
Fat	19.5 g
Carbohydrates	7.8g
Protein	4.3 g
Cholesterol	35 mg
Sodium	696 mg

* Percent Daily Values are based on a 2,000 calorie diet.

Rustic Pancakes II

Ingredients

- 1 1/3 C. milk
- 1 egg
- 1 tbsp applesauce
- 2 tsps ground ginger
- 1 tsp vanilla extract
- 1 tsp ground cinnamon
- 2 C. baking mix
- cooking spray

Directions

- Get a bowl, combine: cinnamon, milk, vanilla extract, egg, ground ginger, and applesauce.
- Add in the baking mix and form everything into a batter.
- Fry 1/4 of a C. of batter in a pan coated with nonstick spray for 4 mins then flip it and cook for 4 more mins.
- Continue frying the batter in this manner until all of it has been cooked.
- Enjoy.

Amount per serving (8 total)

Timing Information:

Preparation	Cooking	Total Time
10 m	10 m	20 m

Nutritional Information:

Calories	134 kcal
Fat	1.8 g
Carbohydrates	24.5g
Protein	4.6 g
Cholesterol	24 mg
Sodium	602 mg

* Percent Daily Values are based on a 2,000 calorie diet.

Asian Style Chicken with Plums

Ingredients

- 1 C. uncooked long grain white rice
- 2 C. water
- 2/3 C. plum sauce
- 1/2 C. light corn syrup
- 2 tbsps soy sauce
- 2 cloves garlic, minced
- 4 packets chicken bouillon granules
- 2 tbsps vegetable oil
- 4 skinless, boneless chicken breast halves - cut into bite-size pieces
- 4 tbsps cornstarch
- 3/4 tsp minced fresh ginger root
- 2 C. snow peas, trimmed
- 1 C. sliced fresh mushrooms

Directions

- Get your rice boiling in water, place a lid on the pot, set the heat to a low level, and let the contents cook for 22 mins.
- Get a bowl, mix: bouillon, plum sauce, garlic, corn syrup, and soy sauce.

- Coat your chicken with cornstarch and then fry it for 7 mins in hot oil or until it is fully done then add in: mushrooms, ginger, and snow peas.
- Cook the mix for 6 more mins or until the veggies are soft then add in the plum sauce.
- Enjoy.

Amount per serving (6 total)

Timing Information:

Preparation	Cooking	Total Time
15 m	25 m	40 m

Nutritional Information:

Calories	432 kcal
Fat	7.4 g
Carbohydrates	70.9g
Protein	20.5 g
Cholesterol	41 mg
Sodium	1283 mg

* Percent Daily Values are based on a 2,000 calorie diet.

Sesame Lemon Shrimp

Ingredients

- 3 lbs jumbo shrimp, peeled and deveined
- 1/2 C. olive oil
- 2 tsps sesame oil
- 1/4 C. lemon juice
- 1 onion, diced
- 2 cloves garlic, peeled
- 2 tbsps grated fresh ginger root
- 2 tbsps diced fresh cilantro leaves
- 1 tsp paprika
- 1/2 tsp salt
- 1/2 tsp ground black pepper
- skewers

Directions

- Get a blender and blend the following: pepper, olive oil, salt, sesame oil, paprika, lemon juice, cilantro, onion, ginger, and garlic.
- Set a little to the side for later.
- Get a bowl, and mix: the wet blender contents and your shrimp.
- Let it marinate in the fridge for 2 hrs. While covered.
- Skewer your shrimp and cook them on a preheated grill or grilling plate for 3 to 4 mins per side.

- While the shrimp cooks make sure you baste it with some of the marinade that was set aside.

Amount per serving (9 total)

Timing Information:

Preparation	Cooking	Total Time
20 m	6 m	2 h 30 m

Nutritional Information:

Calories	286 kcal
Fat	15.7 g
Carbohydrates	3.8g
Protein	31 g
Cholesterol	230 mg
Sodium	355 mg

* Percent Daily Values are based on a 2,000 calorie diet.

LEAN SOY GINGER PORK

Ingredients

- 2 tbsps vegetable oil
- 1/2 inch piece fresh ginger root, thinly sliced
- 1/4 lb thinly sliced lean pork
- 1 tsp soy sauce
- 1/2 tsp dark soy sauce
- 1/2 tsp salt
- 1/3 tsp sugar
- 1 tsp sesame oil
- 1 green onion, diced
- 1 tbsp Chinese rice wine

Directions

- In hot oil cook your ginger for 2 mins then combine in sugar, pork, salt, soy sauce and dark soy sauce and stir fry for 12 mins.
- After 12 mins add in your rice wine, sesame oil, and onions. Let the contents lightly boil until you find that your pork is soft.
- Enjoy.

Amount per serving (2 total)

Timing Information:

Preparation	Cooking	Total Time
15 m	15 m	30 m

Nutritional Information:

Calories	322 kcal
Fat	29.7 g
Carbohydrates	2.2g
Protein	9.4 g
Cholesterol	41 mg
Sodium	838 mg

* Percent Daily Values are based on a 2,000 calorie diet.

Ginger Tofu

Ingredients

- 1 lb firm tofu
- 1 C. fresh orange juice
- 1/4 C. rice vinegar
- 1/3 C. soy sauce
- 1/3 C. canola oil
- 4 tsps dark sesame oil
- 3 cloves garlic, diced
- 1 tbsp diced fresh ginger root
- 1/4 tsp red pepper flakes
- 1 green onions, cut into 1-inch strips
- 1/4 C. coarsely diced fresh cilantro
- 2 dried chipotle chili pepper (optional)

Directions

- Cut your tofu into 4 slices width-wide. Then cut out as many triangles as possible.
- Layer your tofu on a working surface and place some paper towel over them. Place on top of the paper towel something heavy like a skillet and let the tofu drain for 45 mins.
- Get a bowl, mix: red pepper flakes, orange juice, ginger, vinegar, garlic, soy sauce, and oils.
- Set your oven to 350 degrees before doing anything else.

- Place your tofu into a casserole dish.
- Coat the tofu with the marinade. Top with some cilantro and green onions. Take the seeds from your chilies and any stems as well. Put the chilies in the tofu. Cover the casserole dish and let it sit in the fridge for 45 mins.
- Remove some of the liquid of the casserole dish so that only the bottom half of your tofu is covered.
- Cook in the oven for 50 mins.
- Enjoy with jasmine rice.

Amount per serving (4 total)

Timing Information:

Preparation	Cooking	Total Time
25 m		1 h 25 m

Nutritional Information:

Calories	419 kcal
Fat	33.6 g
Carbohydrates	14.6g
Protein	20 g
Cholesterol	0 mg
Sodium	1224 mg

* Percent Daily Values are based on a 2,000 calorie diet.

SWEET SOY CHICKEN

Ingredients

- 1/2 C. hot water
- 1/2 C. creamy peanut butter
- 1/4 C. chili paste
- 1/4 C. soy sauce
- 2 tbsps vegetable oil
- 2 tbsps white vinegar
- 4 cloves garlic, diced
- 2 tsps grated fresh ginger root
- 1/4 tsp ground red pepper
- 3 lbs skinless, boneless chicken breast halves - cut into bite-size pieces

Directions

- Get a bowl, mix: crushed red pepper, hot water, ginger, peanut butter, garlic, chili paste, vinegar, soy sauce, and oil. Put your chicken in this mix. Place a covering on the bowl and place it in the fridge for 8 hrs.
- Heat up your grill or grilling plate and oil it. Skewer the chicken and grill them for 11 mins per side. Make sure the juice of the chicken runs clear after grilling.
- Enjoy.

Amount per serving (8 total)

Timing Information:

Preparation	Cooking	Total Time
10 m	20 m	1 d 30 m

Nutritional Information:

Calories	338 kcal
Fat	16.6 g
Carbohydrates	8.6g
Protein	40.1 g
Cholesterol	97 mg
Sodium	675 mg

* Percent Daily Values are based on a 2,000 calorie diet.

Brown Sugar Ginger Salmon

Ingredients

- 4 (8 oz.) fresh salmon fillets
- salt to taste
- 1/3 C. cold water
- 1/4 C. seasoned rice vinegar
- 2 tbsps brown sugar
- 1 tbsp hot chili paste
- 1 tbsp finely grated fresh ginger
- 4 cloves garlic, diced
- 1 tsp soy sauce
- 1/4 C. diced fresh basil

Directions

- Heat up your grill or grilling plate. Then oil it.
- Coat your salmon piece with some salt.
- Cook it on the grill for about 8 to 10 mins per side.
- Once the salmon is ready it should flake when broken with a fork.
- Get a saucepan, or small pot, and combine: soy sauce, water, garlic, rice vinegar, chili paste, and brown sugar.

- Get the contents boiling then set the heat to low and let it simmer for 4 mins until thick.
- Cover your salmon with this mix and also some basil.
- Enjoy.

Amount per serving (4 total)

Timing Information:

Preparation	Cooking	Total Time
5 m	20 m	25 m

Nutritional Information:

Calories	377 kcal
Fat	13.7 g
Carbohydrates	13.4g
Protein	48.4 g
Cholesterol	100 mg
Sodium	519 mg

* Percent Daily Values are based on a 2,000 calorie diet.

Japanese Inspired Shrimp

Ingredients

- 1 tbsp salt
- 2 C. cold water
- 1 lb shrimp, peeled and deveined
- 1/3 C. chicken broth
- 2 tsps rice wine
- 1 1/2 tsps soy sauce
- 1 1/2 tsps cornstarch
- 3/4 tsp sugar
- 1/8 tsp ground white pepper
- 1 tbsp vegetable oil
- 2 tbsps diced garlic
- 1 tsp diced fresh ginger root
- 2 tsps vegetable oil
- 6 oz. snow peas, strings removed
- 2 tbsps diced fresh chives
- 1/4 tsp salt

Directions

- Get bowl mix: water and salt, then shrimp. Let the shrimp sit in the water for 5 mins.
- Take out the shrimp and pat them dry with paper towels.
- Get a 2nd bowl, mix: pepper, broth, sugar, rice wine, cornstarch, and soy sauce. Place the mix to the side.
- Cook your shrimp in 1 tablespoon of olive oil with high heat in a wok. Stir fry this constantly so no burning occurs for about 1 min. Then add

in 2 more tsps of oil, garlic, 1/4 tsp of salt, snow peas, and chives. Cook for another 1 min.

- Add in your broth and cornstarch and continue stir frying until everything is thick.
- Enjoy hot.

Amount per serving (4 total)

Timing Information:

Preparation	Cooking	Total Time
20 m	10 m	30 m

Nutritional Information:

Calories	207 kcal
Fat	7.8 g
Carbohydrates	7.8g
Protein	24.7 g
Cholesterol	173 mg
Sodium	2172 mg

* Percent Daily Values are based on a 2,000 calorie diet.

Coconut Chicken

Ingredients

- 1 1/2 lbs skinless, boneless chicken breast halves - cut into 1 inch cubes
- 2 limes, zested and juiced
- 2 tbsps grated fresh ginger root
- 1 3/4 C. coconut milk
- 1/2 tsp white sugar
- 1 C. jasmine rice
- 1 tbsp sesame oil
- 1 tbsp honey
- 1/4 C. sweetened flaked coconut

Directions

- Get a bowl, combine: grated ginger, chicken breast, lime zest, and lime juice. Place a covering on the bowl and let the chicken marinate for 30 mins in the fridge.
- Get a saucepan and combine: sugar and milk. Get it lightly boiling then add in your jasmine rice. Set the high to low then place a lid on the pan and cook for 22 mins.

- Get a wok hot with sesame oil and then add in your chicken and the liquid. Cook for 5 mins stirring constantly with high heat.
- Add your honey and keep stirring so nothing burns.
- Shut off the heat and add in your coconut enjoy with rice.

Amount per serving (4 total)

Timing Information:

Preparation	Cooking	Total Time
15 m	25 m	1 h

Nutritional Information:

Calories	660 kcal
Fat	31.2 g
Carbohydrates	53g
Protein	43.8 g
Cholesterol	104 mg
Sodium	117 mg

* Percent Daily Values are based on a 2,000 calorie diet.

RESTAURANT STYLE SCALLOPS

Ingredients

- 2 tbsps thinly sliced green onion
- 2 tbsps butter
- 1 large carrot, julienned
- 2 tbsps diced fresh ginger root
- 1/2 C. white wine
- 1/2 C. heavy whipping cream
- salt and pepper to taste
- 1 1/4 lbs scallops
- 2 tbsps butter

Directions

- Fry your onions in 2 tbsps of melted butter. Then add in your carrots and stir fry for another min.
- Add the wine and ginger. Then some pepper, salt, and cream.
- Keep stirring and heating the contents until half of the liquid evaporates.
- Add your scallops and cook for 1 more min. Finally add the rest of the butter.
- Enjoy.

Amount per serving (4 total)

Timing Information:

Preparation	Cooking	Total Time
15 m	15 m	30 m

Nutritional Information:

Calories	365 kcal
Fat	23.7 g
Carbohydrates	7.4g
Protein	24.8 g
Cholesterol	118 mg
Sodium	336 mg

* Percent Daily Values are based on a 2,000 calorie diet.

Onion Soup

Ingredients

- 2 tbsps olive oil
- 1/2 C. diced onion
- 1/4 C. grated fresh ginger
- 2 cloves garlic, diced
- 4 C. Chicken Stock
- 4 C. sliced peeled carrots
- 1/2 C. evaporated milk (or for an alternative with less fat, use half and half)
- 1/4 tsp ground cumin

Directions

- Fry onions, 1/4 C. diced ginger, and garlic for 9 mins. Then combine in 3 C. of chicken stock and 4 C. of diced carrots. Place a lid on the pan and simmer everything for 32 mins.
- With a batch process blend the soup in a processor or blender and then put the contents back in the pan and get it warm.
- Once everything has been processed and is warm again add in some salt, pepper, cumin and half and half. Enjoy.

Amount per serving (4 total)

Timing Information:

Preparation	Cooking	Total Time
10 m	40 m	50 m

Nutritional Information:

Calories	187 kcal
Fat	9.5 g
Carbohydrates	19.3g
Protein	8.7 g
Cholesterol	9 mg
Sodium	550 mg

* Percent Daily Values are based on a 2,000 calorie diet.

THE BEST BOK CHOY

Ingredients

- 4 heads baby bok choy
- 3 tbsps olive oil
- 1/4 C. water
- 2 tbsps capers
- 1 1/2 tsps diced garlic
- 1 1/2 tsps diced fresh ginger root
- 2 tbsps balsamic vinegar
- 1 dash fresh lemon juice, or to taste

Directions

- Remove the leaves of your bok choy. Dice up the stems. Then dice the leaves. Cook the stems in olive oil for 4 mins. Then add water and the leaves. Cook for 11 more mins.
- Combine in your ginger, capers, and garlic. Cook for 2 more mins. Coat bok choy with lemon juice and vinegar.
- Enjoy.

Amount per serving (4 total)

Timing Information:

Preparation	Cooking	Total Time
15 m	15 m	30 m

Nutritional Information:

Calories	111 kcal
Fat	10.4 g
Carbohydrates	4.1g
Protein	1.7 g
Cholesterol	0 mg
Sodium	195 mg

* Percent Daily Values are based on a 2,000 calorie diet.

RAISIN SALAD

Ingredients

- 4 C. shredded carrots
- 1 C. raisins
- 1/4 C. orange juice
- 1/4 C. shredded candied ginger

Directions

- Get a bowl, nicely mix: candied ginger, carrots, orange juice, and raisins.
- Place a covering on the bowl and let everything sit in the fridge for 8 hrs.
- Enjoy.

Amount per serving (10 total)

Timing Information:

Preparation	Cooking	Total Time
10 m		40 m

Nutritional Information:

Calories	72 kcal
Fat	0.2 g
Carbohydrates	18.3g
Protein	0.9 g
Cholesterol	0 mg
Sodium	33 mg

* Percent Daily Values are based on a 2,000 calorie diet.

Orange Chicken

Ingredients

- 1/2 C. frozen orange juice concentrate, thawed and undiluted
- 3 tbsps fresh lemon juice
- 1/4 C. hoisin sauce
- 1 tbsp vegetable oil
- 1/4 C. sugar
- 3 tbsps diced peeled fresh ginger
- 3 cloves fresh garlic, diced
- 2 lbs chicken wings
- 3 medium green onions, thinly sliced

Directions

- Combine orange juice concentrate, fresh garlic, lemon juice, ginger, hoisin sauce, sugar, and veggie oil in a resealable plastic bag with your chicken wings. Place in the fridge for 8 hrs.
- Cover a baking sheet with some foil. Then set your oven to 400 degrees before doing anything else.
- Cook your wings in the oven for 50 mins on the sheet. Then before enjoying them, top with some green onions.

Amount per serving (4 total)

Timing Information:

Preparation	Cooking	Total Time
20 m	45 m	9 h 5 m

Nutritional Information:

Calories	348 kcal
Fat	15.2 g
Carbohydrates	36.3g
Protein	17.1 g
Cholesterol	48 mg
Sodium	307 mg

* Percent Daily Values are based on a 2,000 calorie diet.

Coconut Soup

Ingredients

- 3 C. coconut milk
- 2 C. water
- 1/2 lb skinless, boneless chicken breast halves - cut into thin strips
- 3 tbsps diced fresh ginger root
- 2 tbsps fish sauce, or to taste
- 1/4 C. fresh lime juice
- 2 tbsps sliced green onions
- 1 tbsp diced fresh cilantro

Directions

- Boil the coconut milk in a big pan. Then add in your chicken strips and simmer for 4 mins with lower heat until the chicken is fully done. Add in your lime juice, fish sauce, and ginger. Heat for 3 more mins then add cilantro and onions.
- Enjoy.

Amount per serving (4 total)

Timing Information:

Preparation	Cooking	Total Time
15 m	10 m	25 m

Nutritional Information:

Calories	415 kcal
Fat	39 g
Carbohydrates	7.3g
Protein	14.4 g
Cholesterol	29 mg
Sodium	598 mg

* Percent Daily Values are based on a 2,000 calorie diet.

CARROT SNACKS

Ingredients

- 1 (12 oz.) package baby carrots
- 1 C. water
- 3 tbsps butter
- 2 tbsps brown sugar
- 1 1/2 tsps ground ginger
- 1/4 tsp salt

Directions

- Boil your carrots in water for 10 mins with a high heat to get everything going and then lower heat for a majority of the time.
- Remove all the liquid then add some butter to the carrots to cover them.
- Combine in: salt, ginger, and brown sugar.
- Get everything simmering again while stirring for about 4 mins.
- Enjoy.

Amount per serving (4 total)

Timing Information:

Preparation	Cooking	Total Time
5 m	15 m	20 m

Nutritional Information:

Calories	134 kcal
Fat	8.8 g
Carbohydrates	14.1g
Protein	0.7 g
Cholesterol	23 mg
Sodium	276 mg

* Percent Daily Values are based on a 2,000 calorie diet.

Sweet Ginger Cornish Hens

Ingredients

- 1/2 C. soy sauce
- 1/4 C. apricot preserves
- 3/4 tsp grated fresh ginger root
- 1 tsp crushed garlic
- 1/2 C. white wine
- 1/2 tsp white sugar
- 2 Cornish game hens, halved lengthwise

Directions

- Get a small dish combine: sugar, soy sauce, wine, apricot, garlic, and ginger. Put in your hens and get them coated nicely. Place a covering on the dish and let the hens sit for 8 hrs in the fridge.
- Set your oven to 325 degrees before doing anything else.
- Put your hens into a casserole dish and cover them with the marinade. Cook in the oven for 1 and 20 mins. Make sure to baste the chicken multiple times.
- Enjoy.

Amount per serving (4 total)

Timing Information:

Preparation	Cooking	Total Time
15 m	1 h 15 m	9 h 30 m

Nutritional Information:

Calories	348 kcal
Fat	17.8 g
Carbohydrates	16.9g
Protein	23.9 g
Cholesterol	128 mg
Sodium	1876 mg

* Percent Daily Values are based on a 2,000 calorie diet.

CHILI BEEF

Ingredients

- 1 tbsp vegetable oil
- 1 1/2 lbs boneless beef sirloin steak, cut into thin strips
- 1 onion, sliced
- 3 cloves garlic, diced
- 3 large celery rib, thinly sliced crosswise
- 3 tbsps diced fresh ginger root
- 2 tbsps soy sauce, or to taste
- 1 tsp chili oil, or to taste
- 6 hoagie rolls, split lengthwise

Directions

- Fry your steak strips in veggie oil until browned nicely but a bit pink the middle. Then add your garlic and onions and cook for 2 more mins. Then add in your celery and ginger and cook for 4 mins.
- Finally combine in soy sauce, and hot chili oil. Place the meat on some rolls.
- Enjoy.

Amount per serving (6 total)

Timing Information:

Preparation	Cooking	Total Time
25 m	15 m	40 m

Nutritional Information:

Calories	605 kcal
Fat	20.2 g
Carbohydrates	72g
Protein	31.1 g
Cholesterol	61 mg
Sodium	1126 mg

* Percent Daily Values are based on a 2,000 calorie diet.

PESTO CHICKEN

Ingredients

- 2 lbs skinless, boneless chicken breast halves
- 1/2 C. dry white wine
- 1/4 C. vegetable oil
- 2 tbsps grated fresh ginger root
- 2 cloves garlic, diced
- 1 tbsp salt
- 1 tsp white sugar
- 1 bunch green onions, cut into 1/4-inch pieces

Directions

- In a sauce pan combine salt water, rice wine, and chicken breast. Get everything boiling then set the heat to low and cook for 10 mins until the chicken is fully done. Place the chicken to the side.
- Cook the following in some veggie oil: sugar, ginger, salt, and garlic.
- With low heat cook the garlic until it becomes soft and browned for about 20 mins.
- Add in some green onions and cook for 10 more mins.
- Slice up your chicken and place it on a plate for serving then top with green onions mix.
- Eat with some cooked rice. Enjoy.

Amount per serving (8 total)

Timing Information:

Preparation	Cooking	Total Time
15 m	30 m	45 m

Nutritional Information:

Calories	201 kcal
Fat	9.2 g
Carbohydrates	3.5g
Protein	22.6 g
Cholesterol	59 mg
Sodium	926 mg

* Percent Daily Values are based on a 2,000 calorie diet.

CRANBERRY PECAN BRUSSEL SPROUTS

Ingredients

- 1/2 lb Brussels sprouts
- 1 tbsp olive oil
- 1/4 C. diced pecans
- 1/4 C. orange juice
- 1/2 C. dried cranberries
- 1 tbsp freshly grated ginger

Directions

- Process your Brussel sprouts in a food processor. Then fry them in olive oil for 6 mins. Set the heat to low and add in your pecans and fry for about 3 mins.
- Add in your orange juice and cranberries and ginger. Let everything cook about 7 more mins before serving.
- Enjoy.

Amount per serving (4 total)

Timing Information:

Preparation	Cooking	Total Time
10 m	15 m	25 m

Nutritional Information:

Calories	154 kcal
Fat	8.5 g
Carbohydrates	20.3g
Protein	2.7 g
Cholesterol	0 mg
Sodium	15 mg

* Percent Daily Values are based on a 2,000 calorie diet.

Indian Tenderloin

Ingredients

- 3 bay leaves
- 1 (1 inch) piece cinnamon stick
- 5 cardamom pods
- 4 whole cloves
- 2 tsps fennel seeds
- 10 whole black peppercorns
- 2 lbs beef tenderloin, cubed
- 3 C. diced onion, divided
- 5 green chili peppers, halved lengthwise
- 1 (1 1/2 inch) piece fresh ginger root, grated
- 6 cloves garlic, diced
- 1/2 tsp ground turmeric
- 1 tsp salt
- 1/2 C. coconut oil
- 1/4 tsp whole mustard seeds
- 4 fresh curry leaves
- 2 1/2 tsps lemon juice
- 1 tsp ground black pepper

Directions

- Grind the following together to make a seasoning: peppercorns, bay leaves, fennel seeds, cinnamon, cloves, and cardamom.
- Get big pot and add in: turmeric, beef cubes, 1 C. of water, garlic, spice mix, grated ginger, 2 C. of diced onions, and green chilies.

- Get everything boiling and then set the heat to low and let the beef simmer for 30 mins.
- Then add in your salt. And let everything continue to cook for 10 more mins, until everything is somewhat dry.
- Place everything to the side.
- Get a frying pan hot with oil, and fry your mustard seeds until they begin to pop, then add in 1 C. of onions that have been diced, cook for 14 mins until they are soft. Then add in your curry leaves and cook for 3 more mins. Add your lemon juice, beef mix, and pepper for 8 more mins.
- Enjoy.

Amount per serving (6 total)

Timing Information:

Preparation	Cooking	Total Time
20 m	55 m	1 h 15 m

Nutritional Information:

Calories	490 kcal
Fat	37.3 g
Carbohydrates	15.6g
Protein	25.1 g
Cholesterol	77 mg
Sodium	450 mg

* Percent Daily Values are based on a 2,000 calorie diet.

THAI STYLE RICE

Ingredients

- 1 tbsp butter
- 1/2 C. uncooked white rice
- 1 C. water
- 1/2 C. hoisin sauce
- 1/2 C. barbeque sauce
- 1 tbsp peanut butter
- 1 1/2 tsps soy sauce
- 1 clove garlic, diced
- 1 tsp grated fresh ginger root
- 2 tsps sesame oil
- 1 C. diced onion
- 1 C. grated carrot
- 2 C. frozen pea pods
- 2 C. frozen diced broccoli, thawed
- 2 eggs
- 1/4 C. sesame seeds, lightly toasted

Directions

- Toast your rice in melted butter then add in water and heat until boiling. Then set the heat to low, place a lid on the pan, and cook the rice for 16 mins.
- Get a bowl, mix: ginger, hoisin sauce, garlic, bbq sauce, soy sauce, and peanut butter. Place everything to the side.
- Once the rice is done get your sesame oil hot until smoking then fry your carrots and onions in it for 2 mins.

- Now combine in your rice and stir fry for 1 min. Add in your peas and broccoli and cook for 2 mins. Add your egg in the pan and scramble with the rice.
- Shut off the stove and put in half of your wet mix. Sample the taste and see if it requires more wet mix. If not half is enough.
- Enjoy.

Amount per serving (6 total)

Timing Information:

Preparation	Cooking	Total Time
25 m	10 m	35 m

Nutritional Information:

Calories	300 kcal
Fat	10.8 g
Carbohydrates	43.2g
Protein	9.3 g
Cholesterol	68 mg
Sodium	731 mg

* Percent Daily Values are based on a 2,000 calorie diet.

CHICKEN AND RICE DONE RIGHT

Ingredients

- 1 C. uncooked jasmine rice
- 1/4 tsp ground turmeric
- 3 tbsps canola oil, divided
- 1 1/4 lbs skinless, boneless chicken breast halves, cut into thin strips
- 1 small eggplant, cut lengthwise in quarters, then crosswise into 1/2-inch-thick slices
- 1 large red bell pepper, cut into 2-inch-long strips

- 1 large onion, cut in half and into 1/2-inch-thick slices
- 2 cloves garlic, diced
- 3/4 C. Swanson Thai Ginger Flavor Infused Broth
- 3/4 C. unsweetened coconut milk
- 2 jalapeno peppers, seeded and diced
- 1 C. fresh cilantro leaves

Directions

- Cook the rice according to its box. Then combine some turmeric with the water.
- Fry your chicken in 1 tbsp of oil until fully done then place the chicken to the side.

- Add the rest of the oil and then fry your eggplants, onions, and red peppers. Cook for 6 mins.
- Add in your garlic and cook for 2 more mins. Finally add in your broth. Set the heat to low and let everything simmer for 9 more mins.
- Blend your cilantro, jalapeno, and coconut milk until smooth. Then add the milk to the eggplants and then combine in your chicken.
- Make sure the chicken is warm and fully done and then enjoy with rice.

Amount per serving (4 total)

Timing Information:

Preparation	Cooking	Total Time
35 m		1 h 15 m

Nutritional Information:

Calories	552 kcal
Fat	22.9 g
Carbohydrates	53g
Protein	33.9 g
Cholesterol	73 mg
Sodium	226 mg

* Percent Daily Values are based on a 2,000 calorie diet.

Couscous Enhanced

Ingredients

- 1 tsp olive oil, or more to taste
- 2 cloves garlic, diced
- 1 1/4 tsps freshly grated ginger
- 1 1/3 C. chicken broth
- 1 C. couscous

Directions

- Fry your garlic and ginger in oil for 2 mins.
- Add in your broth and get everything boiling. Once boiling pour in your couscous. Remove the pot from the stove, and place a lid on it.
- Let the couscous sit for about 9 mins until no liquid is left.
- Enjoy.

Amount per serving (4 total)

Timing Information:

Preparation	Cooking	Total Time
10 m	10 m	20 m

Nutritional Information:

Calories	181 kcal
Fat	1.6 g
Carbohydrates	34.4g
Protein	6 g
Cholesterol	2 mg
Sodium	325 mg

* Percent Daily Values are based on a 2,000 calorie diet.

QUINOA AND GINGER

Ingredients

- 1 tbsp butter
- 1 tbsp olive oil
- 1 onion, diced
- 4 C. chicken broth
- 1 butternut squash - peeled, seeded, and cubed
- 1 (1 inch) piece fresh ginger, peeled and grated
- 1 tsp ground cumin
- salt and ground black pepper to taste
- 2 C. water
- 1 C. quinoa
- 1 tbsp butter

Directions

- Fry your onions in 1 tbsp of melted butter for 11 mins. Then mix in your broth, onions, butternut squash, cumin, and ginger. Let the contents simmer for 22 mins.

- Blend the squash mix in the blender or food processor in a batch process then enter everything back into the pan and add some pepper and salt for seasoning.
- Get a new pan, boil some water and salt. Once boiling add in your quinoa and set the heat to low. Place a lid on the pan and let the contents simmer for 20 mins until all liquid is gone.
- Combine quinoa and soup and some butter as well.
- Enjoy.

Amount per serving (6 total)

Timing Information:

Preparation	Cooking	Total Time
10 m	40 m	50 m

Nutritional Information:

Calories	254 kcal
Fat	8.4 g
Carbohydrates	40.8g
Protein	6.7 g
Cholesterol	14 mg
Sodium	705 mg

* Percent Daily Values are based on a 2,000 calorie diet.

Thanks for Reading! Join the Club and Keep on Cooking with 6 More Cookbooks....

http://bit.ly/1TdrStv

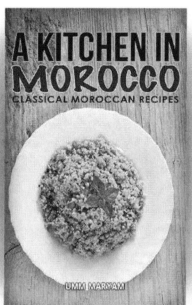

To grab the box sets simply follow the link mentioned above, or tap one of book covers.

This will take you to a page where you can simply enter your email address and a PDF version of the box sets will be emailed to you.

Hope you are ready for some serious cooking!

http://bit.ly/1TdrStv

COME ON...
LET'S BE FRIENDS :)

We adore our readers and love connecting with them socially.

Like BookSumo on Facebook and let's get social!

Facebook

And also check out the BookSumo Cooking Blog.

Food Lover Blog

Printed in Great Britain
by Amazon